THE DECLARATION OF INDEPENDENCE

KATHERINE MANGER

Britannica®
Educational Publishing

IN ASSOCIATION WITH

ROSEN
EDUCATIONAL SERVICES

Published in 2017 by Britannica Educational Publishing (a trademark of Encyclopædia Britannica, Inc.) in association with The Rosen Publishing Group, Inc.
29 East 21st Street, New York, NY 10010

Distributed exclusively by Rosen Publishing.
To see additional Britannica Educational Publishing titles, go to rosenpublishing.com.

First Edition

Britannica Educational Publishing
J.E. Luebering: Executive Director, Core Editorial
Mary Rose McCudden: Editor, Britannica Student Encyclopedia

Rosen Publishing
Nicholas Croce: Editor
Nelson Sá: Art Director
Nicole Russo: Designer
Cindy Reiman: Photography Manager

Library of Congress Cataloging-in-Publication Data
Names: Manger, Katherine, author.
Title: The Declaration of Independence / Katherine Manger.
Description: First edition. | New York : Britannica Educational Publishing in
  association with Rosen Educational Services, 2017. | Series: Let's Find
  Out! Primary Sources | Includes bibliographical references and index.
Identifiers: LCCN 2016023858| ISBN 9781508103950 (library bound)
  | ISBN 9781508103967 (pbk.) | ISBN 9781508103196 (6-pack)
Subjects: LCSH: United States. Declaration of Independence—Juvenile
  literature. | United States—Politics and government—1775-1783—Juvenile
  literature.
Classification: LCC E221 .M146 2017 | DDC 973.3/13—dc23
LC record available at https://lccn.loc.gov/2016023858

Manufactured in China

CONTENTS

PRIMARY SOURCES

A primary source is an artifact, document, or other source of information that was created at the time being studied. Primary sources include speeches, photographs, newspapers, letters, paintings, and even buildings.

   Primary sources are very important to the study of history. They provide a window into the past and give us a firsthand view of historical events. The most accurate information about our history comes from studying primary sources.

A letter that John Adams wrote to Thomas Jefferson is an example of a primary document. Adams and Jefferson helped write the Declaration of Independence.

The Declaration of Independence is on display at the U.S. National Archives in Washington, D.C.

The Declaration of Independence is an important primary source document. It is a piece of evidence from the beginning of the United States of America. Most books and articles about the Declaration of Independence are secondary sources. A secondary source interprets a primary source for its audience.

THINK ABOUT IT

The thirteen original colonies used the Declaration of Independence to formally announce their separation from Great Britain. Why would it be important for the colonies to formally announce their separation with such a document?

What Is the Declaration of Independence?

The Declaration of Independence is the founding document of the United States. The document said that the thirteen original colonies of America were "free and independent states" from Great Britain.

The people in the colonies felt that Great Britain was not treating them fairly. They had protested for

The original Declaration of Independence is securely preserved for public viewing.

many years, but the king would not listen to them. Finally they went to war against the British in 1775. In 1776 they decided to call themselves independent even as the war continued. The Declaration of Independence first lists the complaints against the English king and then makes the actual declaration.

The **preamble** states that there are rules of humankind that are accepted as truths: "That all men are created equal, that they are endowed by their Creator with certain unalienable Rights, that among these are Life, Liberty and the pursuit of Happiness."

An engraving made by printer William J. Stone in 1823 shows the Declaration of Independence (1776).

THE CONTINENTAL CONGRESS

In the early 1770s, citizens of the thirteen British colonies in North America were starting to rebel against Great Britain. A group of patriots called together the First Continental Congress to plan future action. The

George Washington is shown standing at a session of the Continental Congress.

First Continental Congress met in secret in Philadelphia on September 5, 1774. All colonies except Georgia sent delegates, or representatives. George Washington, Patrick Henry, John Adams, and Samuel Adams were among them.

The delegates discussed their complaints about the British. They protested having to pay British taxes without being represented in Parliament. Parliament was the lawmaking body of the British government. The Continental Congress also called for the colonies to boycott, or refuse to buy, British goods.

By 1775, however, they knew that it was time to take more action. The American Revolution began in April of that year.

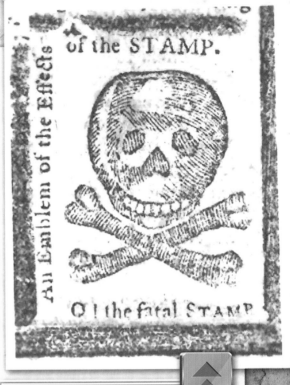

Newspapers and other publications protested against the Stamp Act because the taxes would hurt their business.

Declaring Independence

When the American Revolution began, most colonists were not seeking independence. They simply wanted the British government to listen to their complaints. But as the war continued, many colonists wanted freedom from British rule.

New reasons for independence from Great Britain appeared regularly. In August 1775, Britain's King George III declared that the colonists were rebels and

A painting by Jean Leon Gerome Ferris of Franklin, Adams, and Jefferson.

attacked them. The British attacked the coast of Maine and did great damage in Virginia.

In January 1776, writer and thinker Thomas Paine published a pamphlet called *Common Sense*. It pointed out how the colonists were being mistreated by George III. Many copies of the pamphlet were sold, and support among the colonists for independence grew.

By June 1776 the Continental Congress accepted the idea of independence.

Thomas Paine's words moved many Americans to fight against British rule.

Other Sources

In the pamphlet *Common Sense*, Thomas Paine wrote how the colonists were being mistreated by the king. He wrote, "The blood of the slain, the weeping voice of Nature cries, 'Tis time to part.'"

Other primary sources from that time also show how the patriots felt about the British and about the future. In a speech before the war started, a man named Patrick Henry said, "I know not what course others may take, but as for me, give me liberty or give me death!"

COMMON SENSE;

ADDRESSED TO THE

INHABITANTS

OF

AMERICA,

On the following interesting

SUBJECTS.

I. Of the Origin and Design of Government in general, with concise Remarks on the English Constitution.

II. Of Monarchy and Hereditary Succession.

III. Thoughts on the present State of American Affairs.

IV. Of the present Ability of America, with some miscellaneous Reflections.

Man knows no Master save creating HEAVEN, Or those whom choice and common good ordain.
THOMSON.

PHILADELPHIA;

Printed, and Sold, by R. BELL, in Third-Street.

MDCCLXXVI.

This is the title page from Thomas Paine's pamphlet *Common Sense*.

THINK ABOUT IT

What do these sources have in common? How is it helpful to hear what people at the time were thinking?

Abigail Adams was the wife of John Adams. John Adams was one of the people planning the new country. His wife had questions about the plans. She wrote to him and asked, "If we separate from [Britain], what Code of Laws will be established? How shall we be governed so as to retain our Liberties?"

Abigail Adams wrote to her husband in favor of American independence.

THE WRITERS OF THE DOCUMENT

The Continental Congress appointed a group of five men to write the formal declaration: Thomas Jefferson, John Adams, Benjamin Franklin, Roger Sherman, and Robert R. Livingston. They played important roles in the colonies and in the early years of the new country.

This painting of John Adams is in the National Gallery of Art.

This sculpture of Benjamin Franklin was made in 1787.

Jefferson and Adams both served as early presidents of the United States. Franklin was a scientist, writer, and inventor. He also convinced France to help the colonists during the American Revolution. Franklin and Sherman both later helped write the **Constitution** for the United States. Livingston served in the government of the new country and was a minister to France.

Drafting the Document

Thomas Jefferson wrote the first draft of the Declaration of Independence. John Adams finally convinced Jefferson to write it by telling him "you can write ten times better than I can."

Jefferson began the document by listing a set of rights that are held by all. He wrote that governments have a responsibility to protect those rights. He then wrote about the ways in which King George III had violated the colonists' rights. The violations were the reasons for seeking independence.

Drafting the Declaration of Independence in 1776 (1859) by Alonzo Chappel.

COMPARE AND CONTRAST

How do you think the king and the rest of the people in Great Britain reacted to the Declaration of Independence? How do you think people in the colonies reacted?

When Jefferson was finished, other members of the committee suggested some changes. Then they discussed the document with the rest of the Congress.

The members of the Continental Congress adopted the Declaration of Independence on July 4, 1776. This date is now celebrated in the United States as Independence Day.

The Declaration of Independence was signed in the assembly room of Independence Hall in Philadelphia.

Signing the Declaration of Independence

When the Declaration was adopted, news spread quickly throughout the colonies. Officials in Boston and Philadelphia read the document out loud to people gathered in public places.

The formal Declaration of Independence was signed on August 2, 1776, by members of Congress present on that date. Those who were not there signed later.

Fifty-six men signed the document. The first person to sign it was John Hancock. He was the president of the

John Hancock is shown writing at a desk.

Continental Congress. As the story goes, he signed his name so it was very large to make sure King George III would be able to read it without his glasses.

The Declaration did not mean that the American colonies were independent of Great Britain. It only stated an intention to separate. Complete separation would have to be accomplished by force. Once the Declaration had been adopted, however, there was no turning back.

There are fifty-six signatures on the Declaration of Independence.

"Certain Unalienable Rights"

The ideas in the Declaration of Independence were not new. Thomas Jefferson based them on political **theories** that others had discussed earlier. However, he showed how the ideas applied to the colonies.

The Declaration of Independence says, "We hold these truths to be self-evident, that all men are created equal, that they are endowed

A memorial to Thomas Jefferson stands in Washington, D.C.

This photo shows women picketing at the White House for the right to vote.

by their Creator with certain unalienable Rights, that among these are Life, Liberty and the pursuit of Happiness."

The Declaration of Independence lists "Life, Liberty, and the pursuit of Happiness" as rights that "all men" get from God. However, many people did not enjoy full human rights. Slaves had almost no rights, and women had limited rights. Most slaves did not gain the basic human right of freedom until the mid 1800s. The struggle for women to gain the same rights as men was slow. Women in the United States did not have the right to vote until the early 1900s.

"Tyranny Over These States"

One part of the Declaration of Independence says, "The history of the present King of Great Britain is a history of repeated injuries and usurpations, all having in direct object the establishment of an absolute Tyranny over these

> **VOCABULARY**
>
> **Tyranny** means cruel and unfair treatment by people with power over others.

◀◀ This painting shows King George III of Great Britain.

British troops fired on a crowd of colonists in 1770. The event became known as the Boston Massacre.

States. To prove this, let Facts be submitted to a candid world."

This means that the colonists believed that the king was a tyrant. They believed he was unfit to be the ruler of a free people and that he had done many terrible things to the colonists over a long period of time. The colonists believed that George III was cruel, unfair, and unjust. To prove this, the Declaration of Independence includes a long list of all the offenses committed by the king. This long list of injustices explains why the colonists wanted to separate from Great Britain.

"To Throw Off Such Government"

The Declaration of Independence states, "It is their right, it is their duty, to throw off such Government, and to provide new Guards for their future security.
— Such has been the patient sufferance of these Colonies; and such is now the necessity which constrains them to alter their former Systems of Government."

This means, it was the "right" and the "duty" of the colonists to revolt against King

George III is remembered as the British king who lost the American colonies.

George III and create a new government. The right of revolution protects people against tyranny. It is the duty of the people to overthrow a government that acts against their common interests.

This passage in the Declaration of Independence makes it clear that the thirteen colonies wanted to separate from the British Empire and the rule of King George III.

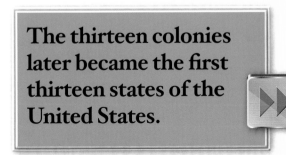

The thirteen colonies later became the first thirteen states of the United States.

COMPARE AND CONTRAST

England was a monarchy, ruled by a king. The United States was formed as a democracy, led by a president. How are a king and president similar? How are they different?

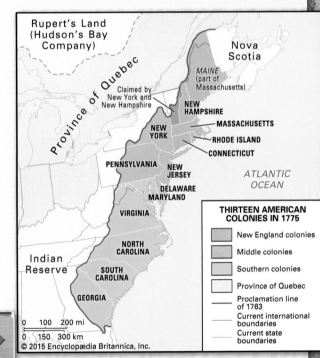

Rupert's Land (Hudson's Bay Company)

Nova Scotia

Province of Quebec

MAINE (part of Massachusetts)

Claimed by New York and New Hampshire

NEW HAMPSHIRE

MASSACHUSETTS

NEW YORK

RHODE ISLAND

CONNECTICUT

PENNSYLVANIA

NEW JERSEY

DELAWARE

MARYLAND

ATLANTIC OCEAN

VIRGINIA

Indian Reserve

NORTH CAROLINA

SOUTH CAROLINA

GEORGIA

THIRTEEN AMERICAN COLONIES IN 1775

New England colonies

Middle colonies

Southern colonies

Province of Quebec

Proclamation line of 1763

Current international boundaries

Current state boundaries

0   100   200 mi
0   150   300 km
© 2015 Encyclopædia Britannica, Inc.

"FREE AND INDEPENDENT STATES"

The final paragraph of the Declaration of Independence states, "These United Colonies are, and of Right ought to be Free and Independent States; that they are Absolved from all Allegiance to the British Crown, and that all political connection between them and the State of Great Britain, is and ought to be totally dissolved; and that as Free and Independent States, they have full Power to levy War, conclude Peace, contract Alliances,

George Washington served in the colonial army and later was the first president of the United States.

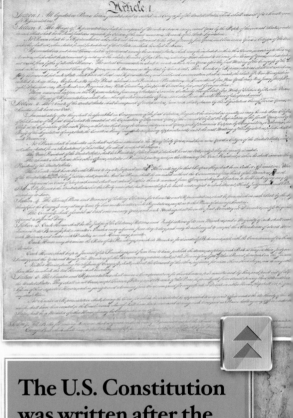

establish Commerce, and to do all other Acts and Things which Independent States may of right do."

This means that the colonies were setting themselves up as an independent country that had the power to defend itself, or "levy War." The new country also had the right to partner and trade with other nations, or "contract Alliances" and "establish Commerce."

The U.S. Constitution was written after the United States became an independent nation.

The Declaration of Independence has since become a source of pride for the American people. It is a reminder of the nation's founding principles.

July 4, 1776

The Declaration of Independence was adopted by the Continental Congress on July 4, 1776, a date celebrated in the United States as Independence Day. The official copy was later written out on parchment and signed by members of Congress.

When the Declaration was adopted, racing horsemen and the noise of cannon fire carried the news far and wide. General George Washington had the document read to the army, and its ringing sentences strengthened the morale of his troops.

On July 8, 1776, the people of Philadelphia gathered at the State House (later renamed Independence Hall) to

Fireworks are an important part of Fourth of July celebrations.

THINK ABOUT IT

The Declaration of Independence became official on July 4. After that the document was written on parchment, and it was signed on August 2. Why do you think the congressmen waited to sign the document?

Independence Hall is where the Declaration of Independence was adopted.

hear a reading of the Declaration of Independence. They were called together by the ringing of the Liberty Bell in the belfry of the building.

Glossary

artifact An object created by people that shows the characteristics of a particular time period or way of life.

belfry A tower or a room in a tower where a bell or set of bells hangs.

candid Marked by or showing sincere honesty.

committee A group of people who are chosen to do a particular job or to make decisions about something.

declare To make known openly or officially.

delegate A person sent with power to act for another.

democracy A form of government in which people choose leaders by voting.

human rights Basic rights that belong to everyone. Some of the most basic rights are the right to live and the right to believe what one chooses.

independent Not being controlled or ruled by another.

intention An aim or purpose.

monarch A person who reigns over a kingdom or empire.

parchment The skin of a sheep or goat prepared as a writing material.

pride A reasonable and justifiable sense of one's own worth.

pursuit The act of going after something.

rebel Being or fighting against one's government or ruler.

revolution The usually violent attempt by many people to end the rule of one government and start a new one.

representative Someone standing or acting for another, especially as an elected official.

session A formal meeting.

sufferance Dealing with suffering or difficulty for a long time.

violations Acts that ignore or interfere with people's rights.

For More Information

Books

Gary, Jeffrey. *Thomas Jefferson and the Declaration of Independence.* New York, NY: Gareth Stevens Publishing, 2012.

Harris, Michael C. *What Is the Declaration of Independence?* New York, NY: Grosset & Dunlap, 2016.

Ransom, Candice F. *What Was the Continental Congress? And Other Questions About the Declaration of Independenc*e. Minneapolis, MN: Lerner Publications, 2011.

Rissman, Rebecca. *The Declaration of Independence* (Foundations of Our Nation). Edina, MN: Abdo Publishing, 2013.

St. George, Judith. *The Journey of the One and Only Declaration of Independence.* New York, NY: Penguin, 2014.

Websites

Because of the changing nature of internet links, Rosen Publishing has developed an online list of websites related to the subject of this book. This site is updated regularly. Please use this link to access the list:

http://www.rosenlinks.com/LFO/declar

INDEX